YA 958.1 DOW
Downing, David, 1946-
Afghanistan

W9-AJL-108

KILGORE MEMORIAL LIBRARY YORK, NE 68467

# AFGHANISTAN

## David Downing

**Marshall Cavendish**
Benchmark
New York

This edition first published in 2009 in the United States of America by
Marshall Cavendish Benchmark.

Marshall Cavendish Benchmark
99 White Plains Road
Tarrytown, NY 10591
www.marshallcavendish.us

All rights reserved. No part of this book may be reproduced or utilized in any form or by any means electronic or mechanical including photocopying, recording, or by any information storage and retrieval system, without permission from the copyright holders.

All Internet sites were available and accurate when sent to press.

First published in 2008 by
MACMILLAN EDUCATION AUSTRALIA PTY LTD
15–19 Claremont Street, South Yarra 3141

Visit our website at www.macmillan.com.au or go directly to www.macmillanlibrary.com.au

Associated companies and representatives throughout the world.

Copyright © Macmillan Education Australia 2008

Downing, David, 1946-
    Afghanistan / by David Downing.
    p. cm. –(Global hotspots)
    Includes index.
    ISBN 978-0-7614-3177-0
    1.Afghanistan–History–20th century–Juvenile literature. 2.Afghanistan–History–2001-
    –Juvenile literature.I. Title.
    DS361.D69 2009
    958.1–dc22

                                                        2008018683

 Produced for Macmillan Education Australia by
MONKEY PUZZLE MEDIA LTD
The Rectory, Eyke, Woodbridge, Suffolk IP12 2QW, UK

Edited by Susie Brooks
Text and cover design by Tom Morris and James Winrow
Page layout by Tom Morris
Photo research by Lynda Lines
Maps by Martin Darlison, Encompass Graphics

Printed in the United States

**Acknowledgments**
The author and the publisher are grateful to the following for permission to reproduce copyright material:

Front cover photograph: Supporters of Osama bin Laden protest against American President George W Bush at a pro-Taliban demonstration in 2001. Courtesy of Getty Images (Per-Anders Pettersson).

Corbis, pp. **4** (David Bathgate), **12** (Ric Ergenbright), **13** (Michel Philippot/Sygma), **17** (Reuters), **19** (Reuters), **20** (David Bathgate), **23** (Reuters), **24** (US Air Force/epa); Getty Images, pp. **6** (Aurora), **8** (Time & Life Pictures), **9** (Hulton Archive), **10** (Hulton Archive), **11** (AFP), **14** (Hulton Archive), **15** (Time & Life Pictures), **16**, **18** (AFP), **21** (AFP), **22** (AFP), **25**, **26**, **26**, **27**, **28**, **29**; iStockphoto, p. **30**.

While every care has been taken to trace and acknowledge copyright, the publisher tenders their apologies for any accidental infringement where copyright has proved untraceable. Where the attempt has been unsuccessful, the publisher welcomes information that would redress the situation.

1   3   5   6   4   2

# CONTENTS

**Glossary words**

When a word is printed in **bold**, you can look
up its meaning in the Glossary on page 31.

# ALWAYS IN THE NEWS

Global hot spots are places that are always in the news. They are places where there has been conflict between different groups of people for years. Sometimes the conflicts have lasted for hundreds of years.

## Why Do Hot Spots Happen?

There are four main reasons why hot spots happen:

1 Disputes over land, and who has the right to live on it.

2 Disagreements over religion and **culture**, where different peoples find it impossible to live happily side-by-side.

3 Arguments over how the government should be organized.

4 Conflict over resources, such as oil, gold, or diamonds.

Sometimes these disagreements spill over into violence—and into the headlines.

### HOT SPOT BRIEFING

**AN ISLAMIC COUNTRY**
The **Islamic** religion (Islam) was brought to Afghanistan by Arabs in the mid-600s. Over the next 200 years, most Afghans became Muslims, followers of Islam. The Afghan culture is centered on this religion.

Residents of Kabul, the capital of Afghanistan, gather at a mosque near the city center. The women are wearing burqas—a type of traditional Islamic dress.

# Afghanistan

Afghanistan has been a hot spot since the 1970s, when the first of several **civil wars** began. Since then, Afghans have continued to fight Afghans. Some want a more modern way of life. Others want to keep their traditional Islamic lifestyle. Many people want a mixture of the two.

# Outside Impact

Foreign countries, such as Russia and the United States, have sent armies to help different groups of warring Afghans. Often they have made things worse rather than better. Also, international **terrorists** and drug dealers have been able to operate from Afghanistan because of weak government control.

## HOT SPOT BRIEFING

### RULING FROM KABUL

The Afghan capital of Kabul is more than 3,000 years old. Governments based in the city have always had trouble extending their control across the whole country.

Afghanistan is a medium-sized country in central Asia. It has land borders with six other countries, but no sea coast.

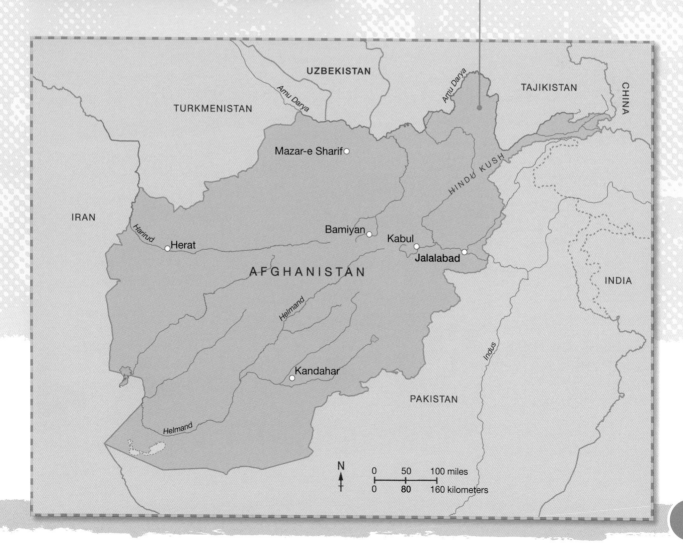

# A REMOTE COUNTRY

Afghanistan is a remote place. There are mountains in the center of the country, deserts to the south and west, and high valleys to the north and east. Afghan summers are hot and the winters are cold. There is very little land suitable for agriculture.

## Life on the Land

Afghanistan has never been a rich country. Traditionally, most people worked in:

- sheep farming on the higher ground
- crop-growing on small valley farms
- trading in the towns.

Today, most Afghans still make a living farming what land they can in the countryside.

> "It's one mass of mountains and peaks and glaciers, and no Englishman has been through it."

A description of Afghanistan in *The Man Who Would Be King* (1888), a short story by the English author Rudyard Kipling.

Heavy winter snow makes road travel impossible in many mountain areas. Some people use animals, such as these yaks, to help them cross difficult land.

# Different Peoples

Among the Afghan people there are several large **ethnic groups**. Each group has its own language. The Pashtuns form just under half of the population. The Tajiks, Uzbeks, and Hazara make up most of the rest. Islam is the main religion for all of these groups.

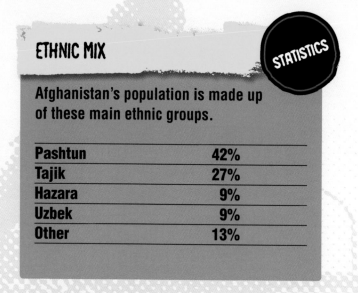

## ETHNIC MIX

STATISTICS

Afghanistan's population is made up of these main ethnic groups.

| | |
|---|---|
| Pashtun | 42% |
| Tajik | 27% |
| Hazara | 9% |
| Uzbek | 9% |
| Other | 13% |

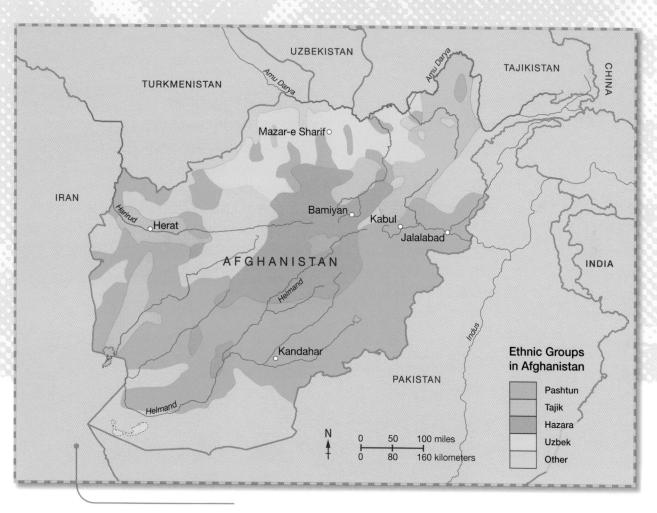

Ethnic Groups in Afghanistan
- Pashtun
- Tajik
- Hazara
- Uzbek
- Other

As this map shows, the Pashtuns live mostly in the east and south of Afghanistan. The Tajiks, Uzbeks, and Hazara live in the center, north, and west.

# A LAND BETWEEN TWO EMPIRES

In the 1800s and 1900s, Afghanistan and the rest of central Asia became a battleground between the British and the Russians. The British were moving north from their **empire** in India. The Russians were moving south from home. Both were worried that the other would seize the land between them.

## Lack of Help

Afghanistan had no rich resources, so Britain and Russia eventually agreed to leave it alone. This meant that, unlike most other poor countries, Afghanistan was not **colonized** by a European power. No one helped the Afghans to improve their roads or railways, better their education system, or run their country in a **democratic** way.

**HOT SPOT BRIEFING**

**DICTATORS**
Until 1978, Afghanistan had a history of powerful individual rulers. They were called either king, khan, or president, but all were **dictators**. Afghan citizens had little say in how their country was run.

British troops in Afghanistan in about 1880. During the 1800s, Britain invaded Afghanistan twice. Both times the Afghans defeated them.

## Future Outlook

By the 1960s, most of the world's poor countries had won back power from their colonial rulers. They were looking forward to **economic** and political progress. Afghanistan, though, was struggling. It had few trading links with the rest of the world. Poverty was widespread. Most children received little schooling, and a small ruling group had political control.

STATISTICS

## A VERY POOR COUNTRY

In 1966, the average Afghan produced goods worth around $70. The average American produced goods worth around $3,500–50 times as much.

A shepherd boy wanders in the Afghan desert. By the early 1970s, people across Afghanistan were starving as they struggled to grow or buy food.

# REVOLUTION

Many Afghans could see that their country was falling far behind the rest of the world. After **World War II**, the spread of international air travel, radio, and telephone lines showed them how life was lived in other countries. Change was on its way in Afghanistan.

## Differing Ideas

Many Afghans became determined to **modernize** their country. They wanted better jobs, education, improved technology, and a fairer political system. Other people benefited from the way things were, and so resisted change.

> "If the peasants eat grass, it's hardly serious. They're beasts. They're used to it."

A Ministry of Agriculture official, speaking of the starving in 1972.

The dictator Mohammad Daoud Khan ruled from 1973 until 1978. He did not keep his promises to modernize Afghanistan.

## The Communists

The best-organized group in favor of modernization was the Afghan Communist Party. This political group wanted:

- more education for both men and women
- a transfer of land to the poor
- equality for women
- less power for the Islamic church leaders.

## Communist Take-Over

In April 1978, a well-known Communist was killed. When a large crowd gathered for his funeral, the government panicked and began arresting other Communists. In response, the Communists began a revolution. They fought until they had overpowered the government and killed the ruler, Daoud Khan. Then they set up a new government of their own.

### HOT SPOT BRIEFING

### COMMUNIST AIMS

Communists want to make society more equal. They believe that everyone should have good housing, clothing, food, and opportunities, and that no one should be very poor or very rich.

Supporters of the Communist government march in Kabul in April 1979, to celebrate the first anniversary of the 1978 revolution.

# THE COMING OF CIVIL WAR

The Communist government introduced changes. Under its rule, both men and women would learn to read and write. Poor people would pay less to **moneylenders** and landowners. Some land would be taken from the rich and given to the poor. These changes upset many Afghans.

## Against the Changes

The idea of women being equal to men did not fit with traditional Islamic belief. Many people were against a government that seemed to be antireligious. The local Islamic leaders, who were often landowners and moneylenders, lost money as the Communists helped the poor. Islamic leaders got together to oppose the new government.

"Privileges which women, by right, must have are equal education, job security, health services, and free time to raise a healthy generation for building the future of the country..."

Anahita Ratebzad, writing in the Communist *New Kabul Times*, May 28, 1978.

An Afghan family sorts grain in 1974. Farmers like these had little money and were forced to pay rent to far wealthier landowners. The Communists believed that this was unfair.

# Civil War

Through 1978 to 1979, discontent turned to violence. Bands of Islamic fighters, called mujahideen, sprang up across Afghanistan. Most ethnic groups formed their own bands, but all agreed that they were fighting for Islam. The mujahideen attacked government troops in the countryside. They even took temporary control of some towns. Civil war had begun.

**HOT SPOT BRIEFING**

**MUJAHIDEEN**
The literal meaning of the Arabic word mujahideen is "strugglers." It is used to describe Muslims involved in a violent struggle against non-Muslims.

Mujahideen soldiers stand in prayer in 1980 while on patrol near the Afghan–Pakistani border. The mujahideen fought under the command of their ethnic group leaders.

# FOREIGN INTERVENTION

In the world outside Afghanistan, a conflict known as the cold war had taken hold. Whenever fighting broke out in a small country, the two superpowers, the Soviet Union and the United States, tried to gain influence by supporting one side or another. They did the same in Afghanistan.

## Soviet and American Support

The Soviet Communists began giving economic help to the Afghan Communist Party soon after the 1978 revolution. When civil war began in 1979, the United States secretly began a program of **military assistance** to the mujahideen. They did this not to support Islam, but to oppose the Communists. The Soviets responded by sending in armed forces to help fight against the mujahideen.

### HOT SPOT BRIEFING

**THE COLD WAR**
The cold war (1947–1989) was partly a power struggle between the democratic, US-led "West" and the Communist, Soviet-led "East." It was also a war of ideas about how to organize economies and governments.

A Soviet tank rolls through an Afghan village in January 1979, ready to support the Communist government.

## Arab Support

A third force also joined in the Afghan civil war. The Muslims of Saudi Arabia felt that supporting the mujahideen against the Communists was an Islamic duty. Their government gave a lot of money, and many individual Saudis went to fight alongside the mujahideen. One of them was Osama bin Laden, the future leader of the al-Qaeda terrorist group.

### AMOUNT OF ASSISTANCE

STATISTICS

At their peak, there were about 120,000 Soviet troops helping the Communists in Afghanistan. Between 1979 and 1989, the mujahideen received around $3–4 billion in assistance from the United States.

These Afghan mujahideen are armed with weapons supplied by the Americans.

# THE SOVIETS ARE DEFEATED

At first, the Soviet armed forces had no trouble seizing control of Afghanistan's towns and the roads that connected them. They had better weapons than the mujahideen. However, they failed to gain control of the rest of Afghanistan.

A mujahideen stands on the shell of a captured Soviet tank in the Afghan city of Jalalabad in 1989. The last of the Soviet troops left Afghanistan in February of that year.

## Soviet Failure

The Soviets struggled to fight in Afghanistan's mountains, deserts, hard-to-reach valleys, and remote villages. The mujahideen ambushed Soviet patrols and then disappeared into the countryside they knew so well. Frustrated, the Soviets relied on bombing from the air. This killed many **civilians** and increased Afghan support for the mujahideen. By 1988, the Soviets realized that they could not win, so decided to leave.

"The helicopters and airplanes come... I am seized by an uncontrollable trembling ... a feeling of total powerlessness."

French nurse Arielle Calemjane, working in Afghanistan, July 1984.

# Fighting Goes On

The Afghan Communist government lasted for another three years. It still had some support among the Afghan people. The Soviets continued to supply money and weapons. At the same time, the mujahideen groups began disagreeing over what sort of Afghanistan they wanted.

## HOT SPOT BRIEFING

**MONEY FROM DRUGS**
During the years of fighting with the Soviets, the mujahideen began producing more than three times as many **opium poppies** as before. These were used to make drugs, which the mujahideen sold to pay for their struggle.

The Afghan Communist leader, Muhammad Najibullah, meets with the Soviet Communist leader, Mikhail Gorbachev, in 1990. In 1992, Najibullah resigned from office.

# ANOTHER CIVIL WAR

In April 1992, Afghanistan's Communist government finally collapsed. The mujahideen now controlled the country. Despite their disagreements, the different groups of mujahideen decided to form a new joint government. This took office immediately.

Gulbuddin Hekmatyar and Ahmad Shah Massoud attend a meeting called in 1992 to heal differences between the mujahideen groups.

## Fighting for Control

Relations between the different mujahideen groups soon broke down. War began again within weeks. For the next three years, the Pashtun, Uzbek, Tajik, and Hazara mujahideen armies strengthened their grip on areas they already controlled. There was bitter fighting in places, such as the capital Kabul, where no one had control. No group was strong enough to defeat the others and take over the whole country.

### HOT SPOT BRIEFING

**SOME FAMOUS MUJAHIDEEN**
The best-known mujahideen leaders were:
- Gulbuddin Hekmatyar, a Pashtun
- Ahmad Shah Massoud, a Tajik
- Abdul Rashid Dostum, an Uzbek
- Abdul Ali Mazari, a Hazara.

# A Country in Ruins

By 1995, Afghanistan had been at war for sixteen years. Most schools and hospitals had been destroyed and towns were in ruins. The amount of food grown had been cut by two-thirds. At least one million people had died and 1.5 million were disabled. Afghans desperately wanted peace, and were ready to support anyone who could provide it for them.

STATISTICS

## LAND MINES

By 1996, there were an estimated 10 million or more unexploded land mines in Afghanistan. These remained a danger, left over from the years of war.

A boy and girl cycle past the war-torn ruin of Darulaman Palace in Kabul. Between 1992 and 1996, the city often changed hands between the warring groups.

# THE TALIBAN

During the years of civil war, millions of Afghan **refugees** had fled for safety in neighboring countries. In Pakistan, some of these refugees formed a new and very extreme group of Islamic fighters called the Taliban. Around 1994, the Taliban began to return to Afghanistan.

## Taliban Control

The Taliban fought for control of Afghanistan. By 1996, they had won all but the far north of the country. Many Afghans welcomed the Taliban because they ended the fighting between rival groups. Many others disliked the strict version of Islamic law that they enforced. Anyone breaking Taliban rules was punished severely. Executions were common.

**HOT SPOT BRIEFING**

**SOME TALIBAN RULES**
The Taliban banned:
- music, TV, and many other entertainments.

They ruled that girls and women:
- could not be educated, work outside the home, or go out without a male relative
- had to cover themselves from head to toe in the burqa.

Kite flying, a traditional Afghan pastime, was banned by the Taliban who said it distracted people from worship. They burned kite shops to the ground.

## Western Disapproval

The Taliban's approach, particularly their treatment of women, produced an outcry in the West. This disapproval grew in 2001, when the Taliban destroyed the world-famous Buddhas at Bamiyan. Afghanistan became isolated from the rest of the world.

**HOT SPOT BRIEFING**

**THE RELIGIOUS POLICE**
The Taliban created a police force to enforce their extreme Islamic laws. It was called the Department for the Promotion of Virtue [goodness] and Suppression of Vice [bad habits].

One of the two giant Buddhas at Bamiyan, built in the 500s CE. The Taliban decided that the historic statues were anti-Islamic and destroyed them.

# THE AL-QAEDA TERRORIST ORGANIZATION

From around 1987 to 1988, two Arab Muslims who had come to fight in Afghanistan's wars founded the terrorist organization al-Qaeda. Osama bin Laden and Abdullah Azzam enlisted many mujahideen fighters in their new organization. These men were trained in terrorist techniques and then sent to fight in other countries where Islam seemed under threat.

## The American Enemy

In 1989, Azzam was killed. The following year, bin Laden returned home to Saudi Arabia. There, he found large American military forces, who had come to protect the kingdom and its oil from neighboring Iraq. Bin Laden considered the forces' presence an insult to Islam. The United States became his main enemy.

"The United States has been occupying the lands of Islam in the holiest of places, the Arabian peninsula, plundering its riches, dictating to its rulers, humiliating its people, terrorizing its neighbors."

Extract from al-Qaeda's declaration of war, issued on February 23, 1998.

Osama bin Laden, speaking in Afghanistan. Bin Laden believes that all Muslim countries should be run under strict Islamic law, like that enforced by the Taliban.

## Return to Afghanistan

In 1996, bin Laden journeyed back to Afghanistan. He arrived just in time to help the Taliban seize power in Kabul. In return for his assistance, the Taliban gave him permission to organize his terror campaign against the West from bases in Afghanistan.

## Terror Attacks

In 1998, al-Qaeda agents bombed two U.S. embassies in Africa. The Americans suspected bin Laden, but the Taliban refused to hand him over. Three years later, on September 11, 2001, al-Qaeda agents killed almost 3,000 Americans and other foreigners in attacks on New York and Washington D.C. These attacks came to be known as "9/11."

### HOT SPOT BRIEFING

### TERRORISTS
Terrorists are people who use violence to frighten their opponents. Since 9/11, al-Qaeda has been the world's best-known terrorist organization.

This video screen grab shows recruits at an al-Qaeda training camp in Afghanistan. Between 1996 and 2001, many hundreds of volunteers passed through these camps.

# THE INVASION OF AFGHANISTAN

After 9/11, the U.S. government gave the Taliban two choices. They could either hand over Osama bin Laden and the other al-Qaeda leaders, or see Afghanistan invaded. The Taliban refused to hand anyone over, so an invasion was planned.

## Attack Tactics

Many countries supported the United States in its decision to invade Afghanistan. Fewer people approved of the way the invasion was carried out. The United States concentrated on bombing from the air to avoid injuring its own troops. More than 1,000 Afghan civilians were killed in these attacks. The United States's Afghan **allies**, the Northern Alliance, did almost all the fighting on the ground.

"The Taliban must act, and act immediately. They will hand over the terrorists, or they will share their fate."

President George W. Bush, September 20, 2001.

### HOT SPOT BRIEFING

**THE NORTHERN ALLIANCE**
The Northern Alliance was an army made up of Tajik, Uzbek, and Hazara mujahideen, who had been pushed back to the north of Afghanistan by the mainly Pashtun Taliban.

Three U.S. Air Force bombers fly in formation during a training exercise.

## Invasion Results

The invasion of Afghanistan had various outcomes. The Taliban were removed from power and a new government was set up. The Taliban and al-Qaeda leaders had escaped capture and disappeared into the mountains.

In addition, the deaths of so many civilians convinced many Afghans that the United States was not a friend of Islam.

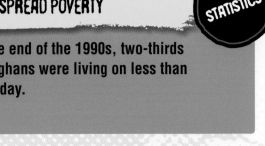

### WIDESPREAD POVERTY

STATISTICS

At the end of the 1990s, two-thirds of Afghans were living on less than $2 a day.

Citizens cheer as Northern Alliance fighters ride their tanks through Kabul, having driven out the Taliban.

# A NEW BEGINNING

Early in 2002, a temporary government was set up in Kabul to replace the overthrown Taliban. The Tajik, Uzbek, and Hazara groups of the Northern Alliance showed they were willing to put the whole country first by allowing a Pashtun, Hamid Karzai, to lead this government. He became president of Afghanistan in 2004.

## Foreign Assistance

The United States and its allies realized that defeating the Taliban was only a beginning. They knew that it would take many years to end the distrust between Afghanistan's warring groups. In December 2001, the **United Nations** (UN) had set up an International Security Assistance Force (ISAF) to help keep the peace. Following Karzai's election win, they hoped that this force would enable his government to extend its control across the whole country.

"Today, Afghanistan has the most progressive constitution [political system] in our region, which enables the Afghan people to choose their leadership for the first time in their history."

Afghanistan President Hamid Karzai, September 22, 2006.

In November 2004, Hamid Karzai makes his victory speech as he is elected president of Afghanistan.

# New Hope

While Afghanistan remained an Islamic country under Karzai, the Taliban's extreme version of Islam was abandoned. Schools for girls were reopened and music played again in the streets. The millions of refugees who had fled the country during the long years of war began to return.

STATISTICS

## REFUGEES

In December 2001, an estimated 3.5 million Afghans were living outside their country, mostly in neighboring Iran and Pakistan.

## HOT SPOT BRIEFING

### WOMEN IN POWER

When elections were held to create a new National Assembly [part of the government] in 2005, women were allowed to vote and stand for office. Several were elected.

Afghan girls return to school in 2002, after six years of being banned from learning by the Taliban.

# THE LONG HAUL

Afghanistan remains a major hot spot. It is still a poor country, and the Karzai government does not yet have control over large areas. The United States and its allies have 40,000 troops in the country. They are there to keep the peace, but their presence still angers Afghans.

## The Taliban Return

Many Afghans see the presence of foreign forces as an **occupation** of their country. Violent opposition is growing, particularly in the south, where a reborn Taliban becomes stronger each year. By 2007, large areas of the southern countryside and several small towns were once more under Taliban control.

### TALIBAN COMEBACK

By the end of 2007, the Taliban had groups of fighters in more than half the districts of Afghanistan.

STATISTICS

British soldiers arrive in the desert of Helmand, southern Afghanistan. Western forces are striving to help overcome the Taliban and restore peace across the country.

## Future Needs

Afghanistan's future depends on how willing others are to help in the years to come. In order to improve life for ordinary Afghans, richer countries need to produce the money they promised in 2001 and 2002 to repair the Afghan economy. They will also need to enforce the Afghan peace for many years to come, if the country's divisions are to have any chance of healing.

"When a person is thirsty he wants water. Afghans are thirsty for unity and peace. We are sick of war."

Shamurat, a village headman.

### DRUG TRADE

STATISTICS

Illegal drugs make up over one-third of Afghanistan's **Gross Domestic Product**. By 2007, Afghanistan was producing more than 92 percent of the world's heroin.

These Afghan workers are scraping opium sap out of poppy heads. Opium is an illegal drug and is used to make heroin.

# FACTFINDER

## GEOGRAPHY

**Capital** Kabul

**Area** 250,000 square miles

(647,500 square kilometers)

**Main rivers** Amu Darya and Harirud

**Climate** Arid to semi-arid. Cold winters and hot summers

**Land use**   Farmland 12%

Other 88%

## PEOPLE

**Population** 31,890,000

**Rate of population change** +2.6% per year

**Life expectancy** 44 years

**Average age** 17.6 years

**Religions**   Muslim 99%

(Sunni 84%, Shi'ite 15%)

Other 1%

**Ethnic groups**   Pashtun 42%

Tajik 27%

Hazara 9%

Uzbek 9%

Other 13%

**Literacy**   Men 43%

Women 13%

## THE ECONOMY

**Agricultural products** Opium, wheat, fruit, nuts, wool, meat, sheepskins

**Industries** Textiles, soap, furniture, shoes, fertilizer, cement, hand-woven carpets, natural gas, coal, copper

**Main exports** Opium, fruits and nuts, carpets, wool, cotton, animal skins, gems

**Gross Domestic Product per person*** $1,000

**National earning by sector**   Agriculture 38%**

Industry 24%

Services 38%

(**excludes opium production)

* Gross Domestic Product per person is the total value of all the goods and services produced by a country in a year divided by the number of people in the country.

(Source for statistics: *CIA World Factbook*, 2008)

**The flag of Afghanistan**

# GLOSSARY

**allies** supporters

**civilians** people who are not soldiers

**civil wars** wars between different groups in the same country

**colonized** ruled by a foreign power

**culture** things that make a group of people distinctive, such as their language, clothes, food, music, songs, and stories

**democratic** giving people regular chances to vote for their government

**dictators** rulers who exercise full power over their people, often in a cruel or ruthless way

**economic** to do with money and the making and distributing of goods and services

**empire** large group of countries ruled by a single country

**ethnic group** group sharing the same race, culture, and/or language

**Gross Domestic Product (GDP)** total value of what a country produces in goods and services in a year

**Islamic** based on Islam, one of the world's major religions, which was founded by the Prophet Mohammed in the 600s

**military assistance** the giving of some or all of the following: weapons, money for weapons, weapons training, and military intelligence

**modernize** bring up to date by making use of the latest ideas and technology

**moneylenders** people who make money by lending it to others

**occupation** (of a country) rule by a foreign power and its troops

**opium** an illegal drug made from opium poppies and used to make other illegal drugs, such as heroin, and the medicinal drug morphine

**refugees** people forced to leave their homes, usually by fighting

**terrorists** person or people using violence to scare others

**United Nations** organization set up after World War II that aims to help countries end disputes without fighting

**World War II** worldwide conflict that lasted from 1939 to 1945, in which Soviet, America, Britain, and others defeated Germany, Italy, Japan, and others

# INDEX